Balance in Christian Living

by
John Noble

Grosvenor House
Publishing Limited

This book is published by
Grosvenor House Publishing Ltd
Link House
140 The Broadway, Tolworth, Surrey, KT6 7HT.
www.grosvenorhousepublishing.co.uk

A CIP record for this book
is available from the British Library

ISBN 978-1-83975-261-2

"We seek to take God 'at His Word' in order to reach out to the lost, to live and love like Christ and to equip disciples of the Lord Jesus as children of Almighty God." **athiswordministries.com**

Contents

FOREWORD

The topic of Balance in Christian Living is of fundamental importance for the born again believer. When we think about the word *balance* we could imagine a set of scales weighing up two sides equally in order to get an even distribution of something. This is a helpful visual aid for this topic when we understand that the Christian faith is not on one side of the scale but is the scale by which our life is measured.

As Christians, the Lord Jesus Christ has met the requirements of the law by His very life on the cross and we are now 'free' in Christ. However, we are not free to live like the world...we are free *from* that and free *for* Christ. This is why the Word of God is the very foundation of all that we seek to do as Christians. How easy it is for the Christian to take the license we have as Christians as the platform to live like the world. How easy it is for the Christian to take the command for obedience as the platform for adding rules on top of what is Scriptural which becomes the deadly vice of legalism. We need balance.

In this book my father (John Noble) is unpacking a number of crucial topics from Scripture in order to enable us to do just that. This is not a book that will make us feel comfortable, and yet the comfort of Christ's saving work is paramount to the Biblical challenges that John sets out in this timely book. I have also been helped to take time to reflect on some of the practical challenges that are laid out in relation to my conscience. We are called to live our lives, doing all to the

Glory of God (*1 Corinthians 10:31*) and there will be different applications from person to person and it is my prayer that this book will stimulate a more Christ-centred focus to people's chief end, which is the Glory of God.

This is a short, challenging, uplifting, Bible-centred book and I highly recommend that you take time to read it through, think and pray about what is being written, what is being asked, and what the Lord is calling you to do in order to get balance in the Christian life.

Pastor John-William Noble
Grace Baptist Church Aberdeen
Author of 'The Basics of Christianity'

CHAPTER 1
INTRODUCTION

How do we get the balance of our lives "right" as Christians in the modern world?

Our Lord Jesus prays for His followers in John 17:14-15 - *"I have given them your word, and the world has hated them because they are not of the world, just as I am not of the world. I do not ask that you take them out of the world, but that you keep them from the evil one."*

This is a powerful and passionate prayer of our Lord Jesus and it means that born again Christians are spiritually reborn and yet still live in this world. Therefore, this leads to many important practical questions that will be considered in this book.

For instance, many will ask how "holy" should we aspire to be? How "worldly" can we be while still living to please Him (2 Corinthians 5:9)? What is God's place in our lives? How can we live for God and His Glory in a world where so many things take up our time? How can we work towards serving God while being part of this world?

How do we get the "right" balance in our worship, our prayer life and our service for God?

We need to consider these things deeply. We need to pray for God's guidance. We need to pray seriously for Him to teach us how to be discerning in evaluating our lives.

Hosea 14:9 - *"Who is wise? Let them realize these things. Who is discerning? Let them understand. The ways of the LORD are right; the righteous walk in them, but the rebellious stumble in them."*

We live in a world where people are striving. Some strive for more power. Some strive to be faster. Some strive to be richer. Some strive to accumulate possessions. Some strive for other people's approval. Some strive for beauty. Some strive for worldly knowledge. Some strive for the latest thing in technology. Some strive for pleasure. Some strive for improved performance. Some strive for fame.

How many strive to know the living God? How many strive to read and study His Word? How many strive to obey Him?

This is not a book advocating monasticism or asceticism. It is certainly not a book advocating "saved and do as we like". It is not a book that gives a magic formula that will suit everyone in finding the 'right balance' in their Christian life in their circumstances.

It is a book that will give us some considerations about finding appropriate balance in the Christian life, by seeking the guidance from God Himself through His Word and the person of the Holy Spirit. It is a book encouraging us to enjoy God's Creation without neglecting God's purposes in our lives. It is a book which seeks to explore how God through His Word and Holy Spirit can help us learn to continuously develop Godly discernment in a way that enables us to be part of this world but at the same time striving to do God's Will for us in our lives.

1 John 4:1 - *"Do not believe every spirit, but test the spirits to see whether they are from God, because many false prophets have gone out into the world."*

How do strike the right balance in our prayer life?

How do we find appropriate balance in worship?

How do we find real joy in our lives?

How do we listen to God?

How do we serve God?

How can we be honest in a world where conformity often goes hand in hand with duplicity and deception?

What TV shows and which films are appropriate and acceptable for us to watch?

How far should we be part of the world and how far removed from it?

There is no "one size fits all" formula for all Christians, but God is there to guide us in our particular circumstances. Are we seeking His guidance? Are we open to being led into the way He wants us to live today and in the future?

God has given us good things as part of His creation. Many of these things can be good or bad depending on how we "use" them and whether they push God out of the centre of our lives or whether these things affirm our faith in our great God. Finding the balance that draws us to the latter of these two should be the focus of our prayers.

Balance in the Christian life is seeking an equilibrium and a spiritual stability that sees us living and enjoying this world in ways that affirm and glorify God. We sometimes think balance is exactly half way between two extremes but that may not always be the case. We must be careful about 'extremes'. Extremes can be bad, but not always. In addition to this, who judges what is extreme and what is not? We must guard against blindly accepting the current values of the world, which are, in nearly every case, ungodly ones. Are we equipped to make such a judgment about what is extreme and where the God-guided choices should fit in?

How do we become equipped to make this judgment? To be equipped we must turn to God and His Word to be guided and given Godly discernment. Immerse ourselves in the Bible. Read it every day. Reflect upon it. Discuss it with others. Pray for God to give us wisdom and direction based upon it. God will guide by His Word. He may also use circumstances at times to make a path clearer in our lives. God never promises that the Christian life will be easy. Nor does He promise to give us all the answers directly or immediately, but He will help us find the answers gradually as He builds us up in growing Godly character through good times and difficult times. He does this through a developing spiritual relationship with Him. This relationship is rooted in the Word of God, motivated and stimulated by prayer and inspired by the Holy Spirit in our lives. This relationship helps us to grow in spiritual life, discernment and love for our great Saviour Jesus Christ.

CHAPTER 2
SPIRITUAL WORLD and MATERIAL WORLD

The Christian life can be a struggle. It can be a compromise. How do we judge where to draw the lines we should not cross? How do we become effective Christians in the world? How much do we need to understand and experience in the world to be effective?

An important starting point is that there are strong guide-lines in God's Word, but the application of these may correctly be a little different for different people in individualised situations. God has given us His Word. He has given us the Holy Spirit to apply His Word for our understanding. God has also given us a brain, gives us wisdom and understanding to guide us along in spiritual and practical discernment along with Christian friends and church leaders.

Galatians Ch.5 vv.22,23 "*But the fruit of the Spirit is love, joy, peace, forbearance, kindness, goodness, faithfulness, gentleness and self-control. Against such things there is no law.*"

In this text the Apostle Paul gives us a list of vital characteristics for the Christian which he calls the 'fruit of the Spirit' given to us by the Holy Spirit. It is not the case that these will be evident in the life of the Christian in equal measure. God wants us to co-operate with Him to receive goodness and have the fruit of the Spirit in us. We can try to have love, joy, peace, patience, kindness, goodness, faithfulness, gentleness, and self control but the Spirit will apply His gifts to our character depending on His Will. It is too hard to do it on our own, we need the Spirit to help us with these things. Let us consider what each of the fruits of the Spirit means.

We begin with love. Think of someone who loves you without condition. You can make mistakes and it doesn't matter what you look like, but they still love you. God loves His children too, no matter what, he even loves you more than your husband/wife, parents! He can help us love others the way we should. Love is difficult at times, but remember that love must be about actions, not just feelings because love is built upon the truth of God's love for us. We show love by how we help others.

1 John 4:19 *" We love because He first loved us."*

The next fruit is joy. Joy is like being very happy, it's being happy inside even when things aren't going great. Joy is a deep sense of 'peaceful happiness' or 'coherent well-being' which is often not connected with our immediate situation or surroundings or relationships. Again, we can *try* to be joyful but only God can give us the kind of happiness which makes us joyful. We can't simply be joyful on our own. Joy is not about false smiles. Joy is not about pretending everything is wonderful when it is not. Joy is an inner peace and assurance, knowing that Jesus loves us and died for us and understands our weaknesses and problems. Joy is knowing that God cares, God loves, God has a plan for our lives which is the absolute best and right plan. Joy is linked to inner assurance that we are God's and He is ours.

1 Peter 8:9 *"Though you have not seen him, you love him; and even though you do not see him now, you believe in him and are filled with an inexpressible and glorious joy, for you are receiving the end result of your faith, the salvation of your souls"*

(We will learn much more about joy from these verses in Chapter 10.)

When we think of peace we usually think of no more fighting or war. That is fair enough, but the peace of the spirit is a bit different. This is the inner peace we gradually come to sense and understand when we get to know God well (by reading the Bible, praying, involving Him in decision-making, etc). If we have this peace we will have a calmness inside and know that all our sins are confessed and that God forgives us. This comes from the assurance that our salvation depends on God, not us.

Psalm 29:11 *"The LORD gives strength to his people; the LORD blesses his people with peace."*

Patience is a tough one for me personally!

Have you ever been told to have patience? How annoying that can be at times! The patience God is talking about is regarding waiting for the big things (and sometimes the small things), to be patient for answers to prayer that might take years to be answered. Patience also, most importantly, involves a trust in God that He will deliver His best in His time. This is not a patience that leads to laziness but to working for God while waiting. It is not a patience of blackmail where we say to God that "we will do *x* for Him if and when He does *y* for us." It is a patience of trust, a patience of action in other areas in line with God's guidance. It is a patience that rests in His Word, studies His Word, persevering in prayer.

Habakkuk 2:3 " *For the revelation awaits an appointed time; it speaks of the end and will not prove false. Though it linger, wait for it; it will certainly come and will not delay.*"

The next fruit is kindness and it should be easy to understand and yet not always so natural to apply, though it should be for the Christian. How easy is it to be kind to e.g. someone who has been mean to you, or to a beggar on the street?

When God gives us this gift, it's more than just being kind to others. He might help us be kind to someone who really needs it and we are not even aware of it. For example, maybe you feel like you should write a letter or call or visit a relative or friend. God might be urging you to do that because they are having a bad day and that's exactly what they need to cheer them up. Sometimes your kind deed to someone else is all they need to remember that someone special loves them. Speaking kindly to people, even those we do not like, builds up relationships with God's creatures as we should.

We can show kindness to people, Christians and others, who we never see or know personally. Prayer and responsible charitable giving can be important acts of kindness towards others in this regard.

Colossians 3:12 *"as God's chosen people, holy and dearly loved, clothe yourselves with compassion, kindness, humility, gentleness and patience."*

Being good (or goodness), is the next fruit of the Spirit.

Having the gift of goodness means God can depend on us to be honest, repent of our sins, and turn away from bad things.

We also need to try to act this way towards others through our actions so they can see the fruit in us. The only true goodness we have is the goodness of God living in us. Doing the right thing even when we really do not want to do it. Do others see this in us?

Romans 12:9,21 *"Love must be sincere. Hate what is evil; cling to what is good. Do not be overcome by evil, but overcome evil with good."*

The next fruit is faithfulness. Being faithful is keeping your promises, being loyal even when times get tough, being trustworthy and doing the things you said you would do. The mother of my current Pastor made a commitment when she was young to pray for her persecuted brothers and sisters in Christ around the world. She has been praying over many decades for a large number of specific individuals who have been persecuted for their faith in Jesus. She keeps detailed notes to make her prayers more meaningful.

Are we faithful to our Saviour? Are we reliable? Are we fully committed to the cause of the Gospel, especially in the "non-glory" aspects of God's work? Can our Church really depend on us at all times? Are we steadfast? Or do we pick and choose how and when we might make ourselves available for God's work?

An example of faithfulness for us may be to pray for someone every day or every week. An example of faithfulness would be to do something to support our local church even when we do not want to do it!

God is so faithful to us. How faithful are we to Him? Are we loyal to Him? Is our faith grounded in God's Word? Do we trust God even when things go very wrong in our lives?

Faithfulness also involves obedience to God's laws. Faithfulness brings perseverance.

Deuteronomy 28:1 *"And if you faithfully obey the voice of the LORD your God, being careful to do all his commandments that I command you today, the LORD your God will set you high above all the nations of the earth. And all these blessings shall come upon you and overtake you, if you obey the voice of the LORD your God."*

Gentleness can be misinterpreted but not when gifted by the Holy Spirit. No matter what situation comes up we are supposed to be gentle. That doesn't mean we shouldn't stick up for ourselves. If someone is doing something you know is wrong you should not accept or condone it. In John 7:53 - 8:11 we see Jesus in gentleness and mercy dealing with a woman caught in adultery. the Jewish leaders organise an execution by stoning but Jesus declares that he who is sinless can throw the first stone, thus saving the woman's life. At the end Jesus tells her not to repeat her sin, but the bulk of this passage shows Him dealing with her gently. Being overbearing or aggressive should be avoided if at all possible, however it may be appropriate to speak and act strongly when defending God and His truth if there is no other way to do so.

Philippians 4:5 *" Let your gentleness be evident to all. The Lord is near."*

Like Jesus was with the woman caught in adultery, we should help people to be restored through gentleness which leads to mercy, forgiveness and being drawn closer to God.

The last fruit is self-control and this is a highly important one that links in to the previous eight.

It means to be in control of what we say and do. As sinners who have rebelled against God, we are enslaved to sin and self-control is not something we can possess. However, for the born again Christian, this is now something that can be developed in us with the help of the Holy Spirit. Without self-control we can't do the things we should. For example, when as a youngster, a brother or sister annoys you so much you just want to hit them, we know that we have to control ourselves and not hit them. Being an only child I have never had that problem and thankfully my two sons have always been close to each other. Now they are married and have families of their own and are learning self-control in different ways in their Christian lives.

There are many barriers to self-control. These include anger, impatience and generally a lacking in the previous eight gifts of the Spirit! However, another barrier to self-control, and to the other Spirit gifts, is pride. Too much pride makes self-control difficult, so we need to develop humility along with self-control. Humility does not mean we have to be timid.

2 Timothy 1:7 " For the Spirit God gave us does not make us timid, but gives us power, love and self-discipline."

For all these nine gifts we need help from God to be able to receive, then use the gifts appropriately, properly and effectively. We need to remember that God made us and He is perfect. If you want the fruit of the spirit to be more evident in your life then first you need to ask God to live in you more and more, ask Him to dwell in your heart, and then the more you get to know him the more this will be true as you grow in maturity and holiness.

As our knowledge and love for Him grows our desire to please Him grows and the outward sign of this inner spiritual growth is an outward living of a life shaped by the gifts from God the Holy Spirit.

It is not a quick fix. It is a developing relationship with our God.

It needs regular confession of sin, and openness to his guidance; coming to him in humility, asking, and eventually receiving not only the gifts of the Holy Spirit but also the wisdom to use them for God's Kingdom. This is why there is such a big emphasis on sanctification (our spiritual growth) in the New Testament.

Therefore we may ask; how far should we be part of the world and how far removed from it?

Jesus did not back off from the world in general. Yes, He went away to pray in solitude, but mostly he mixed with current human life and got in among people and understood what they were doing, saying and experiencing. How do we get the balance between the material and the spiritual in this world. Picture old fashioned scales with the two pans on either side. I remember as a teenager having a part-time job which involved, among many other things, filling and weighing out bags of potatoes. I would put a metal weight in one pan and the bag in the other pan, filling up with potatoes until the weight in the two pans was balanced. Is that how we balance the spiritual and material, getting an equal 50 / 50 split? I do not think that is the way to do it, especially as we do not have an accurate measure for that, whether it be measuring our time or our motivation or our actions. The true measure of balance comes only in a personal and deepening relationship with our God. We pray to Him every day, we read His Word every day, we reflect upon the spiritual needs of ourselves and other and take action.

Another interesting aspect of my youthful weighing of the potatoes was that my boss told me to put the larger potatoes at the top of the bag as most people preferred larger ones and if they were at the top of the bag then the customers would be fooled into buying what they thought was a bag full of large potatoes, not seeing the smaller ones underneath. It was a deception I was unhappy with, so I did not do it, and I told my boss why I would not do it. In a similar way some Christians try to mask their huge amount of worldly excess by presenting a few offerings of spiritually acceptable items to the outside world, hoping these will cover up the selfish excesses hidden behind them. Make no mistake, we may fool the world, we may even fool other Christians, but we can never fool God. He sees the small potatoes in the lower reaches of our bag. God knows our lives, our hearts, our thoughts and our motivations.

Psalm 139: 23,24 - *"Search me, God, and know my heart; test me and know my anxious thoughts. See if there is any offensive way in me, and lead me in the way everlasting."*

Let us consider what might be the "things of this world" but which might equally be vital parts of God's great Creation to be used for both material and spiritual benefit. We could take the view that the pleasurable things of this world are part of God's Creation and that is correct in most cases but certainly not all. The good things in life are certainly there because God wants us to enjoy them, but we need to discern what is for our good and the good of others and what is not. What pulls us towards God and what pulls us away from Him? How do we decide what pleasures are God-given and which are sinful? How do we learn to distinguish between good and bad interactions with the modern world? Surely prayerfulness and immersing ourselves in God's Word are crucial to us being open to God's guidance.

The fear of being contaminated by worldly sin should be there, however it must not make us isolate ourselves from the world but instead it should help us be on our guard against being sucked in to many of the vanities of the world. God's Word is our guideline but it is not a guideline that asks us to live in the 1st or 16th or 19th centuries, but to live in the 21st Century as sensible examples to others. It is all too easy to be attracted to the pleasures of this world. The pleasures may be good in small doses but if they replace God they become sinful and spiritually dangerous.

There are a number of practical issues here that are not explicitly commanded in the Bible which then become matters of conscience to the individual Christian. Such issues are very important and some of the following questions and areas are written to help us all think and pray about how we find balance in a way that is pleasing to God and where the fruit of the Spirit is more evident in our lives.

With regards entertainment; what should we watch on TV or Film or DVD or on the Internet or other media? How do we strike a balance between being aware of the direction local, national and international cultures are going, without being contaminated by the sinful aspects? We need to be aware of prevalent sins in the world while striving with God's help from falling into these sins ourselves. If we hear swearing or blasphemous profanities, do we recoil from them or embrace them? Do we ignore them without even thinking? Do we resist them by pretending they don't exist or by steadfastly refusing to use such words ourselves?

We were once sitting drinking coffee in a fashionable and elegant Paris hotel that I can only describe as being full of "civilised sin" which was exhibited in ways that the world would applaud and many people would envy and strive to be part of. Sin may be tawdry and nasty, but it can also be respectable and high class in the world's eyes. Sin is sin. Sin is choosing to deviate from God's Word and God's Will.

How responsible are we with our money? How do we decide what are legitimate treats and what is extravagance? We have a duty of stewardship with our money, to use it wisely and effectively.

Ecclesiastes 5:10 - *"He who loves money will not be satisfied with money, nor he who loves wealth with his income; this also is vanity"*

Money should be seen as a tool which can be used for good or bad. When it ceases to be a tool and we fall in love with money, it can then lead to our lives being distorted and led away from God by being consumed by worldly pursuits.

Do the things we love consume us?

Matthew 6:21 - *"Where your treasure is, there will your heart be also."*

Are we consumed by the love of money or the love of God? Do we use our money responsibly?

Spending money on some of what we like is not wrong if it is balanced. For some people it might be spending money on meals out. For some it might be holidays or clothes. For some it might be houses, including doing them up. For some it might be cars. For some it might be sports or other hobbies. How do we decide what is responsible spending? How many holidays is it reasonable to have? How expensive should our car or cars be? How much should we spend on meals out or other socialising? We need to seek a Godly balance. By that I do not mean that we are totally extravagant then salve our conscience with a bit of God-focused activity. Nor do I advocate greed or stinginess with money. Being careful and sensible with money, including budgeting and planning, is a prudent part of Godly stewardship. Being mean with money is not.

Proverbs 3:9 - *"Honour God with your wealth."*

How do we decide how much we give to God and how we choose, plan and organise that giving? Jesus makes it clear that we are to store up treasures in heaven (Matthew 6:19-24) and we must understand that everything we have belongs to God. However, how do we use our money? How much do we give to the church? What do we need to support our family? It is right and absolutely essential to give to our local church, but it is also right to give to charitable causes that God has laid upon your heart. This might be to support persecuted Christians or the distribution of Bibles or alleviating suffering and poverty in the local community or in the wider world. Jesus gave us plenty of examples of compassion for those in need, both physical and spiritual needs.

Giving to God includes money, but also includes our time and our talents. Are we praying earnestly to God to guide us how we should use our time and talents for Him? Are we praying that He will open up opportunities for us to serve Him, and are we ever ready to walk through any doors He opens for us?

2 Chronicles 16:9 (KJV) - *"For the eyes of the Lord run to and fro throughout the whole earth"*

It is a sobering thought that God's eyes are always upon us. But what kind of eyes are they? Are they judgmental eyes? Are they loving eyes? They are certainly eyes that see into our heart and know what our true love and motivation is.

(1 Chronicles 16:11) - "Look to the Lord and His strength; seek His face always". God loves us and wants to talk with us. He wants to guide us, encourage us, support us, all in ways no-one else can. Do we trust Him enough to open up to Him and ask Him consistently and persistently to direct us in the right path? Are we praying for Him to give us Godly discernment to help strike an appropriate balance in our lives between the spiritual and material aspects of life?

Proverbs 15:14 - *"Who is wise? Let them realize these things. Who is discerning? Let them understand. The ways of the LORD are right; the righteous walk in them, but the rebellious stumble in them."*

CHAPTER 3
PRAYER AND WORSHIP

How should we pray? How long should we pray for? How often should we pray? Why should we pray?

There is no "one size fits all" formula for prayer. However, at the heart of prayer must be a heart for God and a genuine desire to communicate with Him and seek His Will.

Prayer must never be reduced to some nebulous 'take it or leave it' effort. Instead it must be a vital engagement with the living God.

Prayer is a wonderful opportunity for us to come to know God and build a relationship with Him. However we must understand that prayer requires two-way communication. Building a relationship with God is, in some ways, similar to building relationships with people around us, conversations need to go both ways; we talk, and then we listen. It is the same with God. Prayer allows and gives us the opportunity to come before Him in praise and worship, to tell God how we are feeling, ask for guidance, assistance and answers to questions, but it is centrally a vital means by which we learn from Him and seek to know what His will is for us. So we need to listen to Him, mainly by daily reading His Word in the Bible.

Another reason for prayer is for repentance. Jesus died for those of us who repent of our sins, put our faith in Him, following which He gives us His righteousness to make us acceptable to God. Only He can grant us forgiveness for the sins we have committed. Prayer is a means for confessing our sins. The Lord has promised us that "I, the Lord, forgive sins, and am merciful to those who confess their sins with humble hearts."

Prayer helps us find purpose. We should earnestly pray and ask God to help us find purpose in our lives. He has a plan for us and desires to lead and guide us.

Crucially, one of the most important purposes of prayer is to bring our will closer to God's will. Many people pray and then become upset when their prayers are not answered. Even though God loves us, it is not always His will to give us the things we desire. Indeed often God will not give us what we ask for because it would not be the best thing for us, and much later He makes it clear to us why. It may be that He has something better in store for us or that our timing is not God's timing and we may have to wait. We should not put a time limit on God but instead persevere until He answers either by responding positively or by making it clear He is sending us in a different direction.

Another important aspect of prayer, and perhaps how we should start most prayers, is to praise God for who He is and what He has done for us. We should also thank God for good things and pray for others in need.

How do we get started with prayer? We start by considering *who* we are praying to. We consider how great God is, how loving, how merciful, how righteous, how holy He is. This will help us to approach Him with reverence. God is not our "pal" or our "buddy". He is Almighty God who is amazingly willing to listen to us. We are praying to the Majestic and Sovereign God of the Universe who knows and yet loves us. Indeed He loves in spite of knowing in every detail how sinful we really are! Such love! He also loves us so much that He has given us this great gift of prayer.

A crucial, underlying necessity for effective prayer is that what we say to God is said with sincerity and belief and trust. We must also persevere in our prayers. It is not enough to pray once then leave it and this is certainly what we see evidenced throughout Scripture (Genesis 32, Nehemiah 1, Daniel 6). Prayer needs to be a good habit of spending time with God.

How long should we pray for? There is no single "one size fits all people" answer to this. Quality is more important than quantity but quality does not particularly mean eloquence but rather it focuses on what is heart-felt and God-directed. God-directed in two ways - directed *towards* God and directed *by* God.

Private prayer is important. How do we decide on its frequency and its focus areas? It is important to have some prayer habits, e.g. a set time, a daily or weekly list. It is also healthy to offer up ad hoc spontaneous prayers to a God who is always listening. Prayer can increase our awareness of God. Prayer can increase our awareness of, and focus upon, the needs of others. God can use our prayers to tune us into His Will.

Public prayer is also important. It should show reverence to our holy God. We should certainly approach Him in both humility and seriousness. Public prayer, like private prayer, needs to be heart-felt and not ritualistic. I once heard a Pastor (in a church I visited but have not returned to), shout (yes, shout!) a prayer to God in a church service, roaring demands upon God. How sad that was. How disrespectful to God and misleading to the congregation. Before we speak to

God we must consider who we are speaking to, and approach Him with humility and thankfulness.

Also recently, while abroad, I heard a Pastor doing a public prayer while a keyboard player performed so loudly that the prayer was difficult to follow. Prayer is not a performance. Prayer is a focusing of minds towards the person and Will of Almighty God.

Hebrews 12:28 - *"Therefore, since we are receiving a kingdom that cannot be shaken, let us be thankful, and so worship God acceptably with reverence and awe".*

The content of public prayer should begin with God, not ourselves. We can break it up into e.g. Adoration, Confession, Supplication, Thanksgiving and Intercession.

Adoration - Speak to God, aware that we are in His presence, and praise Him for all that He is and all that He has done.

1 Chronicles 16:11 - *"Look to the LORD and his strength; seek his face always."*

Confession - Acknowledge that we have sinned against our God, confess our sins, repent of our sins, seek and receive forgiveness from our merciful God.

1 John 1:9 - *"If we confess our sins, he is faithful and just and will forgive us our sins and purify us from all unrighteousness."*

Supplication - Ask God to encourage us and build us up spiritually.

Romans 8:26 - *"In the same way, the Spirit helps us in our weakness. We do not know what we ought to pray for, but the Spirit himself intercedes for us".*

Thanksgiving - We thank God for the greatness of His person and actions.

Ephesians 1:18 - *"I pray that the eyes of your heart may be enlightened in order that you may know the hope to which he has called you, the riches of his glorious inheritance in his holy people,"*

Intercession - We pray for help for others.

1 Samuel 12:23 - *"As for me, far be it from me that I should sin against the LORD by failing to pray for you"*

It is very important in both private and public prayer that we are guided and influenced by the Bible.

Matthew 26:41 - *"Watch and pray so that you will not fall into temptation. The spirit is willing, but the flesh is weak."*

Prayer should not be self-serving or self-promoting. In some churches there are prayers that all too often speak about how the person or his church will press on or break through or be the seat of revival, and these types of prayers often glorify self instead of glorifying God.

Public prayer is an honour and a responsibility in guiding others towards communing and communicating with the living God. Public prayer is a God-given opportunity to encourage others in their prayers and in their lives.

What is the best way to worship? Are there right or wrong ways to worship?

Psalm 100:1-3 - *"Shout for joy to the LORD, all the earth. Worship the LORD with gladness; come before him with joyful songs. Know that the LORD is God. It is he who made us, and we are his ; we are his people, the sheep of his pasture."*

To some extent the sincerity and belief needed for genuine prayer should hold a key part in all types of worship. How sincere and believing is our worship? How much is it heart-felt rather than just routine or a performance?

Isaiah 29:13 - *"The Lord says: "These people come near to me with their mouth and honour me with their lips, but their hearts are far from me. Their worship of me is based on merely human rules they have been taught."*

Worship Warning - When we try to deny God or try to re-invent Him in our image we go down a seriously wrong path of self-worship.

We must not diminish God in our minds or in our hearts, trying to bring Him down to our level so we can control Him. To do so is to deny who God is.

How great is our desire for heartfelt worship of the living God? How well do we know, and seek to know further, the God we come to worship?

Let us consider musical praise items such as hymns and worship songs.

Old fashioned hymns accompanied by an organ are still liked by some, largely but not exclusively elderly people. Newer worship songs, accompanied by a worship band, are becoming more prevalent and popular with a variety of ages (including myself and others in the over 60 age group). However there is now a tendency to have what I might call performance songs where the band performs a song as if in a concert rather than leading congregational worship.

Worship songs in church should encourage us to reflect on our amazing God and music has the ability to arouse our emotions and passion for our Saviour. It is also very important indeed that the words we sing are meaningful and theologically sound. Unfortunately there is a growing trend in some churches and in some modern worship songs for the lyrics to be repetitive and theologically misleading at times.

It can be very worshipful (showing reverence and enthusiasm for God) to combine a rousing strong-beat music played by a talented, God-focused worship band with lyrics which are meaningful, Biblical and helpful. Equally such worshipful lyrics may also be combined well with a slower and more contemplative tune.

Music and song needs to draw in the worshippers to love, adore and feel a deep passion for their God. Meaningful lyrics displayed on a clear, large screen or screens can also enhance worship with others.

Then there are the physical accompaniments that some relish, such as hands in the air and eyes closed. The question may be why people are putting their hands in the air. Is it to hail the greatness of our God or is it to show off to others how holy they want to be thought of by the observers? I am not a hand-raiser personally but have no objection if it is done to hail God's greatness as opposed to vaunting someone's own self-proclaimed holiness.

Using our voices is the most obvious way to engage in worship but contemporary songs often lend themselves to a more interactive approach in which hands may be raised, people may sway to the rhythm of the music and hand-clapping can be an appropriate accompaniment. These physical gestures may be done in genuine worship and response to our great Saviour, or they may be committed in terms of doing the things that others expect of them rather than in true worship. We should examine why we praise God in the way we do so.

Psalm 95:1 - *"Come, let us sing for joy to the Lord; let us shout aloud to the Rock of our salvation."*

If our worship is from the heart then God is honoured. Pleasing Him and praising Him need to be the purposeful driving force of our worship, regardless of its outward appearance or whether it is traditional or modern. It is good and pleasing to Jesus when we worship Him with our minds, our bodies and our hearts.

Ephesians 5:19 - *"Sing and make music from your heart to the Lord."*

Which are right? Traditional? Modern? Lively? Contemplative? They all could be, and then again none of them might be. What do I mean by that? There is no one right style of worship in terms of musical or physical style, but there is a right type of worship in sincerity and faith and a heart-felt desire to connect with God.

Psalm 150:1-6 - *"Praise the LORD. Praise God in his sanctuary; praise him in his mighty heavens. Praise him for his acts of power; praise him for his surpassing greatness. Praise him with the sounding of the trumpet, praise him with the harp and lyre, praise him with tambourine and dancing, praise him with the strings and flute, praise him with the clash of cymbals, praise him with resounding cymbals. Let everything that has breath praise the LORD."*

How do we worship God? Why do we worship God? Is it not truly amazing that our God chooses us to receive His grace, mercy, forgiveness, salvation and the imputed righteousness of Jesus? We should marvel that God had named us, totally undeserving as we are, as I am, as you are. This is worship and gratitude and prayerfulness based on God's Word. As we further reflect on the Bible and the night before the Crucifixion we can speak of Jesus viewing His last sunset before He died for us - a sunset He created. We can worship the Creator and the Saviour with understanding, reverence and love.

A vital part of worship centres on the Bible and how people are helped to understand it and apply it to their lives. The Bible needs to be read out loud in church while people read the words either in a Bible (preferably) or on a screen. The Bible needs to be read at home every day. We need to speak about the Bible to others.

If we have a relationship with God we will want to read His Word.

If we do not want to read His Word we are spurning a relationship with the living God and with Jesus, who alone can save us from our sins and lift us up into spiritual fulfilment.

2 Timothy 3:16 - *"All Scripture is God-breathed "*.

God will call some to be preachers and teachers. Many people claim to be preachers but a lot of them fail to deliver the inspired message because they are not listening to God and/or learning from Him. I am appalled at how many people who have the temerity to allegedly "preach" but who do not have the calling, the gift, the ability or the depth of character to do so. Preachers are accountable to God not other humans and time should be invested by local churches to invest in the development of men in leadership and to discern those who are gifted and called to preach.

James 3:1 - *"Not many of you should become teachers, my brothers, for you know that we who teach will be judged with greater strictness."*

It is a great responsibility and honour to preach God's Word and it must be done with passion, with knowledge, and with great prayerfulness. Preaching needs to expound, to explain and apply God's Word for the spiritual benefit of the listeners.

2 Timothy 4:1,2 - *"I charge you in the presence of God and of Christ Jesus, who is to judge the living and the dead, and by his appearing and his kingdom: preach the word; be ready in season and out of season; reprove, rebuke, and exhort, with complete patience and teaching."*

Preaching is a calling. Preaching is a gift. Preaching is God's design. Preaching must expound God's Word. Preaching must not exalt us.

Preaching must exalt Jesus. Preaching must teach. Preaching must edify. Preaching must challenge. Preaching must encourage - but it is to be encouragement to follow God's ways not the ways of the world.

Thus it must be grounded in a systematic understanding of the whole Bible. Erroneous theology or ignorance of the whole Bible are unacceptable in a preacher. Unacceptable? Perhaps that is not strong enough, as erroneous theology and/or ignorance of the whole Bible in a preacher or so-called preacher is an insult to God, His truth, and His mighty works. Any pick and mix approach to the Bible is highly dangerous and can lead to making up a wildly wrong theology misleading others in a spiritually damaging way.

So-called preachers who just "tickle the ears" of the listeners with what they want to hear - a "gospel" without responsibility or obedience - are insulting God. They are undermining the Will of God. They are leading their listeners astray. They will have a lot to answer for to God in terms of e.g. their cowardice and pride.

Preachers have to learn. Preachers have to pray. Preachers have to be courageous when a Biblical message may be uncomfortable for listeners. Preachers have to present God in all His glory. Therefore preachers must not be boring! Preachers should be enthusiastic - not about themselves, but about God's mighty Word. Preachers have to preach obedience and service. Preachers have to preach about sin, responsibility, salvation, redemption, resurrection, and all the other great messages in God's Word.

We also need to consider *where* we worship and *why* we worship there.

If we attend a church out of habit, that alone is a poor reason unless it is accompanied by much stronger reasons.

If we attend a church because it does not put pressure on us to examine ourselves and our lives, that is a bad reason.

If we attend a church because the preaching is sound, Biblical, personally challenging and edifying, that is a good reason.

If we attend a church because God is clearly using us in a work there, that is a good reason.

Our church needs clear Biblical doctrine. Why? With clear Biblical doctrine we are drawn closer to God and His Will for us, individually and collectively. Without clear Biblical doctrine a church will ultimately promote a lifestyle where God is marginalised. This is unacceptable. God must be in the centre. God's Word must be proclaimed, expounded, discussed and lived.

Proper balance in a church is *not* moderate or middle of the road. Proper balance in a church is only found through sound Biblical doctrine.

Too many "happy" churches promote a "come as you are, stay as you are, and you can even indulge your sin further if you fancy it" approach cloaked in a highly diluted theology that dishonours God and the whole counsel of His Word. That is not balance. That is an affront and a serious offence to our Saviour. Sin is very serious. How do we know? Look at how seriously Jesus dealt with it on our behalf.

That is why we must seek out a church with strong Biblical doctrine and preaching.

Now if you live in a rural area or small town you may not have much choice of churches. Seek guidance from God in prayer. Many people speak about their "local" church but that does not have to be a church in the same town where you live if that town is without a church with strong Biblical doctrine and preaching.

How do we know if we have found such a church?

Here are a few questions to consider in our search for a God-honouring, Bible-centred, prayerful, caring and mission-minded church.

Is inner repentance encouraged more than outward conformity?

Is the preaching expounding Bible truths and teaching people to learn about, and draw closer to God?

Is prayer a crucial driving force?

Is the church mission focused and active both locally and internationally?

Does the church have a serious attitude to membership and discipleship and spiritual growth?

Is the church led by a godly, qualified man who is inspired by the Holy Spirit? Does the church look to God's Word to decide how the church should be organised and led?

Is the church doctrine clear and true to the whole of Scripture?

Are the members serious about their faith, their Christian responsibilities and in reaching out to other people to bring them closer to God and His truth?

CHAPTER 4
DUTY FULFILLED?

Acts Ch. 23 v.1 *"Paul looked straight at the Sanhedrin and said, 'My brothers, I have fulfilled my duty to God in all good conscience to this day.'"*

Can we say this ? Have we truly fulfilled our duty to God in all good conscience to this day ?

To begin to answer this we need to consider *what* is our duty to God and *why* it is our duty to Him.

Our duty to God needs to be considered in the context of WHO God is, and who we are in RELATION to Him.

God is the source of life, including our life.

God is Omniscient - God knows everything and His knowledge is complete.

God is Omnipotent - God is able to bring about everything that He chooses (but He has chosen to give us free will and our sin brings many problems into the world).

God is Omnipresent - He is present in all places at all times.

God is Immutable - By nature, God is unchanging.

God is Holy - God is set apart, different, perfect.

God is Righteous - God not only does what is right, He is the source of perfection in doing and choosing.

God is Sovereign - God's sovereignty is how He rules His creation. This is what makes Him free to do what He knows is best for us. Though He is in complete control, He has also given us a free will to obey or reject His leading.

God is Love - This also means He wants to grant us His mercy, grace and loving-kindness.

God is Merciful - God's mercy has been defined as God not giving us what we deserve. We, as sinners, deserve eternal punishment away from His presence, yet in His mercy He has chosen to offer us in the sacrificial death of Jesus, a way for salvation, which we can accept by repentance and faith, leading on to serving Him.

This gives us a very small glimpse into who God is.

On the other hand, WE have sinned against this holy and righteous God. We deserve eternal punishment.

But God in His love and mercy has offered us salvation through the work of Jesus.

We owe so much to our God.

So what is our duty to God ? What is our relationship to Him ?

Our duty to God is to acknowledge Him, love Him, serve Him, tell others about Him, pray to Him, ask His guidance, ask Him to be at the centre of our lives.

If we do not tell others about our great God then what does that say about our faith and our attitude towards non-believers. Are we quite happy for non-believers to go to Hell? Are we indifferent on this dire consequence for them? Whether we picture Hell as a huge fiery furnace that burns but does not consume, or view Hell as a series of never-ending, dark hallways, all leading to punishment and everlasting hopelessness, do we care enough to warn others what eternity without God may be like? Surely an eternity without God for anyone must weigh heavily on the minds of every believer. Hell is a reality or a future for millions of lost souls now. Do we care enough about God and other people to try to help others know and experience the love and salvation of our great Saviour? Surely this is an obligation of love upon us.

Think about your relationship with God. What is it really like?

Maybe compare it with the relationship of a husband/wife or parent/child in human terms. If we are in a close relationship with a human being, surely we want to:

- spend time with that person
- do things with and for that person
- speak regularly to that person
- speak about that person to others.

Is that true of our relationship with God? Do we:

- spend time with God?
- do things with and for God?
- speak regularly to God?
- speak about God to others?

How central, is God in our lives? How crucial is God to our decision-making and actions? How far are we striving to live by His Word? Is God's influence in our lives showing through in our sense of justice, our caring, our honesty, our integrity, our witness to others?

Or are we self-centred, hypocritical, just paying God lip-service?

What about our family? Do we want the best for them? "of course we do" you answer. However, if you really mean this then the "best" for your family is to come to know, love and serve Jesus as their personal Saviour. Is this our heart's desire for our family? Is this our heart's desire for our friends? Is this our heart's desire for strangers?

What are we doing to work towards our heart's desire? Are we prayerful, seeking God's Will and asking Him to give us the opportunities and the words to help bring others to the truth and a relationship with the living God?

Do others see that we have a vibrant relationship with the living God?

"Paul looked straight at the Sanhedrin and said, 'My brothers, I have fulfilled my duty to God in all good conscience to this day.'"

Can we say this?

Have we truly fulfilled our duty to God in all good conscience to this day?

What about tomorrow, and the next day, and every other next day?

CHAPTER 5

CHRISTIAN LIFE WITH OR WITHOUT RESPONSIBILITY

This seems a simple choice but it is perhaps more complex than we think. What are the responsibilities of a Christian, and how do we fulfil them?

I was told once that one Christian said to another "I like you but not when you judge me". It sounds fair enough at first sight, but when you find out that what the person really meant was that he/she wanted to do what they liked without accountability or responsibility then we must say that this is an unbiblical stance.

Colossians 3:16 *"Let the word of Christ dwell in you richly as you teach and admonish one another with all wisdom"*

Let us think of the word "responsibility". When I was a Head Teacher and had students in my office for "advice" I sometimes took out a coin and slapped it on the table and asked them if it was a one-sided or two-sided coin. Once we established it was a two-sided coin I told them that for their life there were two sides to what they wanted if they were to succeed in life. The two sides of that "coin of life" were Privilege and Responsibility. They may want all the privileges and rewards, but in order to have a balanced life they needed to live up to their responsibilities.

Responsibility can be seen as a duty, but in terms of the economy of God's grace we might be better looking at responsibility as being hand-in-hand with gratitude.

Many churches seem to promote what I call a "Good-time Gospel". Yes, they advocate being "saved", which is good as far as it goes. However, there is no teaching on an obedient walk with God following the "salvation". They are happy to concentrate on what we are saved *from*, and miss out the life we are saved *to*. It is (wrongly) quite acceptable to 'tick the salvation box' thus ensuring the 'heaven ticket' but then you can live and direct your life as *you* want. The fun Gospel without cost is thus promoted. God's moral compass is ignored. The Lordship of Jesus is denied. The truth is perverted to a lie risking damnation.

Some of these churches describe themselves as "amazing" and "incredible". Perhaps they are "incredible" in so far as they ignore vast swathes of Biblical teaching to suit their own hedonistic desires and to be "popular" with the people. Sin is rendered as something to be confessed once then almost forgotten. The reality is that the closer we get to God the more aware we are of our sin. If we deny our sin we deny God. Jesus died for our sin because it is a serious problem that needed a drastic solution. To belittle sin is to belittle the great self-giving of Jesus on our behalf.

Another worrying trend in these self-proclaimed "amazing" churches is that there is no need for membership. Therefore no responsibility, no loyalty, no commitment. Instead a loose association. You are amazing, you are wonderful, you do not need to commit here - that is their deceptive and unbiblical message.

Joining our local Bible-led church and being accountable to it, committed to it, loyal to it, shows how serious we are about our faith in Jesus.

Grace Baptist Church Aberdeen has this statement on its website - "Every professing believer who is baptised upon profession of faith is then to be added to the local CHURCH. This is not about a place that we go to but a people that we belong to. This people is the bride of Christ who meet together to worship the Lord in fellowship seeking to grow and serve together in faith."

The great privilege and undeserved gift of salvation brings with it a responsibility to obey God and a desire to know more of Him and His standards. The great privilege and undeserved gift of salvation was won for us at tremendous cost by Jesus our Saviour. He suffered physically, mentally, and above all spiritually, for us, who did not deserve such grace and love. How will we respond? We will want to respond in repentance, faith, prayer, service and grateful obedience in commitment to Him and to a local church with sound Biblical doctrine as a guiding focus.

Freedom through obedience is a phrase that seems like an oxymoron, but it is a paradox of Biblical truth that we should strive to apply in the Christian life. Our natural, sinful nature would make us think that obedience is the opposite of freedom, but when it is obedience to God it will free us from sin and its enslaving power and guilt.

James 1:25 *"But whoever looks intently into the perfect law that gives freedom, and continues in it—not forgetting what they have heard, but doing it—they will be blessed in what they do."*

The word obedience comes from the Latin word ob-audire which means to hear or to listen to. Do we want to listen to God?

"Everyone who listens to these words of mine and acts on them will be like a wise man who built his house on rock. The rain fell, the floods came, and the winds blew and buffeted the house. But it did not collapse; it had been set solidly on rock" Matthew 7: 24.

Obedience gives us freedom because it helps us to avoid wallowing in sin, opinion, doubt and error. Jesus said: *"If you love me, keep my commands"* John 14:15, and *"You shall know the truth and the truth shall make you free"* John 8: 32.

Obedience involves acknowledging, accepting and putting oneself under the authority and will of God. It includes both submitting to Him and then expressing that submission in actions, words and thoughts. To be obedient is to yearn to be in agreement with God.

It is important not to confuse obedience with legalism. True obedience is not a nit-picking observance of the letter of the law, but a life becoming tuned in to the spirit of the law, tuned by the Holy Spirit so that we develop Godly discernment with His help.

Let us now consider the dichotomy between "Are You Guys Having Fun in Church?" and our persecuted brothers and sisters.

How (if at all) responsible is it to turn Church worship into a laugh and a joke? Contrast that with the plight of so many faithful believers who endure dreadful suffering but still refuse to deny their Saviour. What is our responsibility to the persecuted Christians? What can and should we learn from them? How do we get the balance right between truly joyful (see chapter 10 on "real joy") worship and a serious prayerful and giving response to, and support for, our persecuted brothers and sisters? As believers washed undeservedly in the saving, cleansing blood of Jesus we **do** have a responsibility to our persecuted brothers and sisters which should be heartfelt and not have to be wheedled out of us reluctantly. What are we going to say to our persecuted brothers and sisters when we meet them in heaven about how we supported them?

Matthew 25:44-45

"They also will answer, 'Lord, when did we see you hungry or thirsty or a stranger or needing clothes or sick or in prison, and did not help you?' "He will reply, 'Truly I tell you, whatever you did not do for one of the least of these, you did not do for me.'

We have a responsibility to our gracious and loving God and part of that responsibility is how we treat others in need.

Matthew 25:40 "Truly I tell you, whatever you did for one of the least of these brothers and sisters of mine, you did for me."

I am not advocating people being miserable in church. There is much to be joyful about. Our heart-felt worship should be because we are happy and grateful to God and devoted to Him. However, we must get the balance right between the serious and the joyful. As I will come to in chapter 10, true joy involves the serious aspects of our faith too. They are not separate sections of worship and service to our gracious God.

Now we come to another serious aspect of the Christian life.

CHAPTER 6
IT WILL NOT BE EASY

Christians will be tested. The testing may come through illness or disappointment or bereavement or failure or frustration. The testing can also come within the church itself. The testing may come when we think God is not responding to our needs - although this may often be because we want a quick answer rather than waiting for the right answer. Patience has never come easily to me and God has often had to teach me patience. Truly trusting in God develops a kind of 'holy patience' that is rooted in the Sovereignty of God in our lives. If we truly accept Him as "Lord" of our lives there will be times we must wait and trust.

Fairly recently I was tested by a series of "unfortunate events" occurring in a very short period of time. Each one of these caused me considerable inconvenience, annoyance, expense and future uncertainty. I was close to "blowing a fuse" on a number of occasions but with the help of my Godly wife I managed to put these events, all of them coming easily into the category of significant injustices, into a more long-term perspective by comparing their effect with other matters which are of far more important consequence in terms of what really matters. So what were the things that really mattered that helped me get my problems and irritations in proper perspective? The important matters included God's Word. God's people and the desire of some of them to commit to spreading the truth about our great Saviour to others.

There are times it can be very helpful to discuss our problems with Godly family or friends. We should not forget the willingness of our Pastor / Minister to help too.

Speaking to people who read, study, understand and apply God's Word can be a source of help, encouragement and finding direction.

Listening to God's Word, reading God's Word, enjoying God's Word and obeying God's Word, are key here.

Luke 6:47 - 49 *"As for everyone who comes to me and hears my words and puts them into practice, I will show you what they are like. They are like a man building a house, who dug down deep and laid the foundation on rock. When a flood came, the torrent struck that house but could not shake it, because it was well built. But the one who hears my words and does not put them into practice is like a man who built a house on the ground without a foundation. The moment the torrent struck that house, it collapsed and its destruction was complete."*

Basing our lives upon God's Word is like building on solid rock. Not living by God's Word is like building with no foundation in life, just waiting to blown away by the life of sin we have so chosen in ignoring God's Word and its authority and power and comfort and direction in our lives.

God's Word can encourage us. God's Word can correct us. God's Word can comfort us. God's Word can inspire us. God's Word can teach us. God's Word can help us to know more of God. God's Word can help us know more of ourselves. God's Word shows us truth.

We like to think as Christians that we are honest and truthful but we are all sinners who are prone to deviating from the truth.

3 John 1:4 - *"I have no greater joy than to hear that my children are walking in the truth."*

Why do we want to tell the truth? Why do we sometimes tell half-truths and lies? It may be to court popularity. It may be out of fear or ignorance or lack of Godly character.

Proverbs 11:3 - *"The integrity of the upright guides them, but the unfaithful are destroyed by their duplicity."*

There are difficulties that may be age-related. When we are young we often have to strive to achieve, strive to be recognised or accepted. When we are older we may find our physical and mental abilities diminishing, and coming to terms with that can be very challenging. Whatever our difficulties in life it is all too easy to use them as an excuse for not getting near to God. We may be "too busy" or "too unwell". There are never times when these excuses are justified. There are never times when we would not benefit from a closer relationship with God. Every day should involve prayer, Bible reading and reflecting on who God is, what He has done for us, and what He can do for us now and in the future.

Do we sometimes have doubts? If we say no, are we saying this out of denial or fear? Doubts that lead us to re-examining our faith and having our faith strengthened can rightly be viewed as good doubts. Unbelief that leads us to ignore God and His Word is very different. Doubt is not the same as unbelief. Working through doubt can strengthen faith as we grow in understanding and in closeness to our God. Unbelief tears us away from God. Our Christian faith is rational but God-given at the same time. When our reasoning struggles, we should pray to God to open our eyes to guide us on to the right path of truth and belief in that truth. Most often He will do this by teaching us through His Word in the Bible.

Even when studying the Bible we must guard against settling for, or choosing only, part of the truth. How easy to just take on board the parts that suit our lifestyle and offer little challenge. We need the complete truth and through that God can bring about growth in our lives.

1 Chronicles 16:11 *"Seek the LORD and his strength; seek his presence continually! "*

When we go through hardship in life we need to go to God in prayer. When things are going well in life we need to go to God in prayer.

Psalm 46:1 *"God is our refuge and strength, an everpresent help in trouble."*

If Christians pretend that the Christian life is easy or that God blesses all the faithful with worldly success and prosperity then they insult God and insult the many Christians who battle for long periods of time in very difficult circumstances.

Romans 12:12 *"Rejoice in hope, be patient in tribulation, be constant in prayer."*

The Christian life involves obeying God. Sounds simple, but it is not.

Acts 5:29 - "But Peter and the apostles answered, "We must obey God rather than men.""

Too often we convince ourselves we are obeying God when all we are really doing is conforming to the compromising, sinful ways of the world. This can even be true in the church. If we accept lukewarm approaches to the opportunities to glorify God we cannot obey God by silently acquiescing. We must strive for Godly preaching, fervent prayer, wholehearted outreach and a spiritually encouraging, Bible focused fellowship.

CHAPTER 7

GOD WORKS FOR OUR GOOD

As we have said there are times we will be tested. At these times we need to remind ourselves that God is working for our ultimate good. What does this mean with regards to our life on this earth? How does this relate to the difficulties we have just considered in the previous chapter?

Romans 8 :28 "*And we know that in all things God works for the good of those who love him, who have been called according to his purpose.*"

This great verse begins with the tremendous proclamation "we know that in all things God works for the good of those who love him, who have been called according to his purpose". It is not to be said quietly or meekly, but PROCLAIMED! Shout it from the rooftops!

The Greek word used for "preaching" in the New Testament is 'kerygma'. This word kerygma means proclamation. It means to let the world know about the good news of Jesus. It means to be enthusiastic in evangelising and teaching. It means to explain through the guiding and inspiration of the Holy Spirit.

So what is Paul proclaiming here? He tells us that we know that God works in all things for the good of...who? Not for everyone, but for "those who love him". But how do we know who are "those who love him"?

Love for Jesus should start at the Cross. We consider what Jesus did there, what He accomplished, why and for whom. We realise that Jesus died to take the punishment for His children. He committed no crime. He chose to take our sins upon Himself, for us, for our benefit. We who sinned against Him do not deserve the suffering Saviour on the Cross dying on our behalf, taking our punishment, dying the death that should be ours. We deserve the punishment. We deserve the suffering. We deserve the death. But God in His mercy provided a way out for us. God Incarnate, Jesus Christ, took our sins upon Himself. As it says in 1 Corinthians 5:21 - *"God made him who had no sin to be sin for us, so that in him we might become the righteousness of God."*

How do we respond to this? We confess our sins, repent of our sins, put our faith and trust in Jesus as our Saviour, and enter a loving, spiritual relationship with Him. This is how we know who loves Him. Those who repent of sins. Those who read His Word every day. Those who pray to Him every day. Those who seek His guidance for their lives. These are the people Paul speaks about in Romans 8:28. For these people he says that *" in all things God works for the good of those who love him".*

Notice Paul does not say that it is all things that work for our good, but GOD working in all things. This not about fate. This is not about accidental occurrences. This is the providential intervention of Almighty God on behalf of His faithful people. However, the good which God works towards is an ultimate good, a long-term outcome, not a short-term quick fix.

God is working "in all things" for our long term good. Let us consider carefully this phrase "in all things". It means all things, both good and bad, pleasurable and painful. God will make all things, good and bad, work ultimately for our good. When we think of the bad things we must not fall into the trap of thinking that bad things, including suffering, are in themselves good. However, God can use them to bring about good at a later time. God can use bad things and turn them into eventual good for us. For example, bad things can waken us up to reality and truth as well as build our character. However, trials and tribulations can also show us our "smallness", weakness and frailty. The world encourages a facade of self-confidence, but it can easily be shattered for individuals. Lessons need to be learned by Christians. We are saved by grace, but often we think we can live the Christian life our way, directed by our desires and we push God's influence to the sidelines. We may be suddenly overwhelmed by an event or a drastic change in circumstances, but God can use this to bring about good for us.

There are many definitions of what is good. Philosophers have argued for centuries about what constitutes good. For the most part, we tend to confuse what is good for us with what we want. However, what we want may often not be good for us. So how can we know what is really good? We can only get closer to knowing by accepting God as the reference point for what is good. Pray to Him. Read His Word. For the truth is that God is the very source of what is good. Goodness is in the character and person of God. Goodness is in the essence of God.

God's purpose for His children is what is good for us. This is far deeper than happiness as defined by the world, namely of a sense of jolliness, jubilation, light-heartedness or euphoria such as many wordly pleasures offer. Our happiness is built upon a true joy, which is found in a growing trust and fulfillment of Him 'working' in us and through us for our good and the good of others and the glory of our gracious God. However, even in the midst of this there may be human suffering.

When suffering comes our way we are prone to question God and at times even unjustly blame Him. It is not fair. Why does God allow it to happen to us?

One very known example of this in Scripture is the suffering of Job in the Book of Job. Job was afflicted. He was described as being like nobody on earth as one blameless and upright, but he was still a sinner. Ultimately he complained bitterly to God. We can sympathise with this, but God's ultimate purpose for good for Job was fulfilled through Job's suffering. His suffering ended and his life took on a new dimension as the quantitative and vast difference between God and man was revealed in a way that aligned Job's heart all the more to the perfect purposes of God in his life for His Glory.

It is often difficult to trust God when life gets tough, but that is when we need to trust Him even more. We also need to develop humility before God. Humility is not defined by 'putting ourselves down', but simply by standing before this perfect God and being convicted of our sinful worthlessness and utter dependence upon His grace for dear life. As a result, we not only see that we need to be forgiven by God, but that we need to rely on His strength and power in our lives. We need to get closer to Him, to become more familiar with the love and grace of God, because our ignorance of God is a barrier to life in its fullness, preventing us from living our lives in completeness through Him. This is because we are too much embroiled in worldliness. It is good to have family, work, pleasures and other worldly things, but not so if we allow them to push God out of the centre of our lives. We must also recognise that God gives all of these things to us, and we can balance our time, commitments and enjoyments with God at the centre of it all, hence why we do everything to the Glory of God (1 Corinthians 10:31). It is why we must be very guarded and pray for wisdom regarding the things of this world lest they become a source of distraction, time wasting or even idolatry. This would undoubtedly become a sin-barrier between us and God, and would cut us off from the good He has in store for us. However, God can is gracious and can and does draw us closer to Him. "We know that in all things God works for the good of those who love him, who have been called according to his purpose." The Christian life is also a learning process.

We are responsible for our decisions in this life and we often make mistakes, but if we repent of our sins and put our faith in Him, He will influence us by His Holy Spirit. We must guard against resisting the work of the Holy Spirit. Remember also that the real power is with God. He works in all things for the good of those who are "called according to his purpose." Our love for God is a response to Him calling us. He calls us - sinners who have sinned against Him. We respond in repentance, faith, love and service. How mindful are we daily of God's presence, God's Word, and God's Will for our lives?

CHAPTER 8
LISTENING TO GOD

It sounds good. We want to listen to God. Do we? Do we really want to listen to God? If we **say** we want to listen to God, do we mean it wholeheartedly or only selectively to suit our own will rather than His Will? Even if we have an initial intention of listening wholeheartedly to God, how will we go about it? How much Bible reading, prayer and talking about God to others are we prepared to do?

Let us consider the words of Psalm 85, including verse 8:

"I will listen to what God the Lord will say"

This Psalm tells us much about God, about ourselves, and what our right relationship with him is / should be.

If we are to find balance in the Christian life then we must listen to God. What is balance for one person may not be for another but God alone can guide us to the right balance for us.

The Psalmist begins in vv.1-3 by listing some of God's past mercies -

How God "showed favour", "restored" his people, "forgave" their iniquity, "covered" their sin, "set aside" His wrath.

God has shown these mercies in the past. The people have sinned again, deserted their God and His Word.

The Psalmist comes (v.4) to ask God: "*Restore us again, O God our Saviour*".

This is a plea of repentance, a plea to receive God's grace and mercy, instead of justice/ deserved punishment.

The plea is continued in v.6 "Will you not revive us again,that your people may rejoice in you".

What is it that makes us happy? We think it is the passing things of this life. But these are mere pale reflections of the glory that is our gracious God.

In verse 7 it says,

"*Show us your unfailing love, O Lord, and grant us your salvation*"

This is love. This is grace. This is power. That Almighty God, though offended by our sin, still loves us, and offers us His gracious salvation.

His love is "unfailing". His salvation is 'granted' - a gift bestowed.

The following verse is then crucial. We need to read it, then decide if we are going to follow it or reject it, and thus reject God.

"*I will listen to what God the Lord will say*"

Are we doing this? Do we want to " listen to what God the Lord will say"? Or are our ears attuned to listening to what we *want* God to say, rather than what He IS saying? If we do listen we are promised "peace", but we are warned not to "return to folly". If we do listen to Him and follow him. i.e. listen and act upon it, we are told in verse 9, "*Surely his salvation is near to those who fear him*".

We need God's salvation. How much we need it. How very much. Our sin, our offence to God, the consequences of our sin: alienation, suffering, spiritual death; all these can only be dealt with by God when we come to repentance and faith in Him.

We like to hear the first part, about God's salvation being near, but look at the second part: "to those who fear him".

'Fear of God' is not terror, it is awe at His righteousness compared to our sin. The Fear of God is engendered by a consciousness and conviction of our own sin, followed by a turning, turning *away* from sin and turning *to* God. While this is vital for salvation, it is also then the reality for the born again Christian. Only if we turn away from sin and turn to God can we begin to receive the blessings of God.

Let us look at verse 10 – "*Love and faithfulness meet together; righteousness and peace kiss each other.*"

This is a picture of God's characteristics, or "attributes", from which we can benefit.

Verse 11 speaks of God's faithfulness.

Verse 12 speaks of God giving His goodness.

Verse 13 returns to His righteousness.

To believe in God, to turn to God, these are essential to having balance, truth and purpose in our lives.

Do we want to do this?

Who do we want to believe in? *Who* do we want to turn to? What kind of God is He? The Apostle Paul prays that the church in Colossae would be *"filled with the knowledge of his will in all spiritual wisdom and understanding,"* (Colossians 1:9) because in order for us to grow in our relationship and experience of God we must have a knowledge of who He is. Thus, the closer we get to Him, the more we read His Word, the more we pray to Him, He will help us develop a healthy and balanced conscience to make balanced decisions on both material and spiritual matters.

When we stand at the judgement, we will all have to listen to what God says. We will not be there to argue our case, but to listen. I once said in a sermon that at the judgement we will not be there to "mouth off at God" but to listen to Him in silence. One extremely arrogant member of the congregation apparently mouthed off quietly against my words because he thought he was so important that God *had* to listen to him!!!! How sad that his pride was blinding Him to who God is and how much we all need Him to forgive our sins.

The glorious news, however, is that when we submit to God in repentance and faith, we receive the salvation won for us by Jesus, bringing us both forgiveness from our sins but also the gift of the righteousness of Jesus to 'clothe' us and protect us.

If we are protected by the righteousness Jesus has imputed to us on account of our faith in Him we will hear that Jesus has covered us, protected us, saved us for eternal life. If we have rejected Jesus we will stand before God's judgement throne on our own to hear the list of our sins and the deserved punishment for them being delivered.

Verse 8 again - *"I will listen to what God the Lord will say"*

Let us be truly honest to ourselves about this. No pretending. Are we listening to the words of God?

Are we really keen to hear His words?

Are we reading His Word every day seeking His Will in our lives?

Are we 'fearing' Him in the sense of awe and wonder at His greatness contrasted with our undeserving sinfulness?

Are we acknowledging our sin, turning from it, turning to God ?

If we are, we can receive His grace. With His wonderful grace come the benefits of a righteous and loving and generous God towards undeserving sinners.

"I will listen to what God the Lord will say" every day. I will seek His Will for me and serve Him with enthusiasm and purpose and delight.

CHAPTER 9
WISDOM FROM GOD

If we wholeheartedly want to listen to God, He is willing to share His wisdom with us. It cannot come in a one-stop "whammy". It must come gradually, for our own good.

1 Corinthians Ch. 1 v. 30

"It is because of him that you are in Christ Jesus, who has become for us wisdom from God - that is, our righteousness, holiness and redemption."

This verse tells us about real wisdom - God's wisdom for us in Jesus Christ. This wisdom will help us find purpose and balance in our Christian life.

Let us break this verse down into three overlapping sections:

1 -"It is because of him that you are in Christ Jesus".......

By the work of God through the new birth, we are now "in Christ Jesus." This wording was used frequently by Paul to describe our relationship with Christ. The word "in," as used in this verse, means a condition, state, or attribute.

The new birth doesn't just produce a changed life but an exchanged life. That is to say, the Lord doesn't make our flesh wise, righteous, sanctified, or redeemed. Instead, *He becomes* our wisdom, righteousness, sanctification, and redemption. When we repent of our sins and put our faith in Him, He forgives our sins and gives us the gift of His Righteousness.

The Christian life is not just difficult to live; it is impossible to live even adequately through our own ability alone. It is only when we cease to operate in our carnal selves and let Jesus live through us that we can obtain victory.

For instance, those who depend on their own intellect *alone* to figure out the direction for their lives will always make mistakes. Many of us think we are intelligent and can work it out ourselves with our great intellect and experience. Such misguided arrogance is all too common. The correct and only way for Christians to act is on the basis that we are fallen sinners who are called to deny ourselves (Mark 8:34) and thus seek and ask God for direction. This is the exchanged life which is now a changed life which is turning away from sin and towards Christ. Therefore, the wisdom of Christ within us will emerge according to God's purpose for us and He will direct our paths. Proverbs 3:6 is a powerful verse and very applicable here,

"Trust in the Lord with all your heart and lean not on your own understanding; in all your ways submit to him, and he will make your paths straight."

2 -"Christ Jesus, who has become for us wisdom from God".

Jesus - our Saviour - our Lord - our imputed righteousness - our Mediator.

Jesus - who loves us, in spite of our sin against Him!

Jesus brings us a wisdom from God that we cannot achieve ourselves. Purely human "wisdom" is flawed by sin and Paul defines this as folly (1 Corinthians 1).

If we receive Christ as Saviour, we identify with Him and we are protected by Him. He brings us His wisdom, which leads to benefits beyond our own power.

But this is a wisdom, although received instead of earned, that we can and must co-operate *with and in*. This is a wisdom, although received instead of earned, that we can and must co-operate *with and in*. Yes, I have repeated that sentence. Why? I have repeated it to emphasise its importance in our continuous search for balance and fulfilment and purpose in the Christian life.

We must learn more about Jesus Christ, deepen our relationship with Him, and be willingly guided by Him. Central to this is to read His Word every day, talk to Him in prayer every day, speak about our Saviour and His Word to others, starting with our own family, then with others.

What does it mean to co-operate "*with and in*" God's wisdom? For the "*with*" it means that we become spiritually united with God, praying often and sincerely to Him, studying His Word and being built up spiritually. For the "*in*" it means that we operate within the direction God gives us through His Word and His Holy Spirit. We serve Him gladly, purposefully and effectively.

3- "wisdom from God - that is, our righteousness, holiness and redemption."

Real Wisdom, bringing with it the righteousness, holiness and redemption of Jesus. This is such a rich offering from our Saviour, but it does not come in an instant fix. It comes through developing our relationship with Jesus and applying His wisdom to our hearts and our lives. Instead of depending on our acts of righteousness to earn the blessings of God, we should accept the fact Jesus, following our repentance and faith, has given us His righteousness. In Christ (or through Christ) is the only way that we can stand before and approach God as 'righteous'. This is another glorious part of God's grace towards repentant sinners - that Jesus imputes His righteousness to us, 'clothing' us in His righteousness, protecting us by His righteousness.

Our spirits are redeemed (see Romans 8:23 - *"Not only so, but we ourselves, who have the firstfruits of the Spirit, groan inwardly as we wait eagerly for our adoption to sonship, the redemption of our bodies."*)... Jesus lives in the spirits of believers, and all His wisdom, righteousness, sanctification, and redemption are ours when we depend on Him instead of on our own abilities. He offers us a wealth of spiritual benefits. Will we come to Him to receive them or pass on the great opportunities He has for us to receive blessing, comfort, challenge, direction and much more?

Wisdom is centred upon the love, knowledge and fellowship of our Lord Jesus Christ. This wisdom can then be applied to our complicated lives in a complicated world. This wisdom can help us assess the balance in our lives and strive with the gracious help of God's goodness.

CHAPTER 10
REAL JOY

Are you happy? Are you really happy?

God is the source of true happiness. Searching for happiness in the things of this world can bring short-term pleasure, but it will not last.

Is it Christian to desire joy and to experience joy? Of course it is!

However, many Christians and many churches mistake joy for forced laughter and a watered-down version of God's Word so we can be happy in leading the life we want, and we want to enjoy. Yes, it's a real good-time gospel in their eyes, but the "joy" they put forward as a preferred style is merely laughing in the face of real joy and sidelining God and His Word to the sidelines.

God created joy, happiness and fulfilment. God is the essential source of joy, happiness and fulfilment. He has a heart for us and that heart is a loving, caring and joyous heart. So where does this joy come from? It comes through believing and knowing God. It comes through a spiritual relationship with Him, grounded in the Word of God, bringing knowledge of God and ourselves, made possible by the saving work of Jesus.

1 Peter Ch.1 vv. 8, 9 *"Though you have not seen him, you love him; and even though you do not see him now, you believe in him and are filled with an inexpressible and glorious joy, for you are receiving the goal of your faith, the salvation of your souls."*

How sensible or joyful is it for us to believe in a God we cannot see with our eyes?

Does it make sense? Can we build our eternal future on it? Is it showing balance in our lives to do so? Are there any other things we believe in without seeing them?

We believe in the existence of the wind. We cannot see it, but we can see its effect, e.g. in the trees, people's hair, etc. Can we "see" the effect of God in action? We believe that after tonight there will be daylight again tomorrow. This is based on past experience transferred to the future. What have we experienced of God in our lives? What is our faith based on?

"Though you have not seen him, you love him; and even though you do not see him now, you believe in him and are filled with an inexpressible and glorious joy, for you are receiving the goal of your faith, the salvation of your souls."

Where is the proof of God's love and salvation?

Where does this proof come from?

This "proof" comes from God Himself and He reveals it to us.

He brings us to repentance and faith. Then He indwells us as the Holy Spirit and gives us experiential proof of His existence, His love, His Salvation, His Power and His Glory.

What of the Christians to whom Peter wrote this to originally?

Though you have not seen him That is, Jesus Christ, whom they had never seen with their human, bodily eyes, when Christ was upon earth, but were scattered about in several parts of the Gentile world; and yet Christ being made known to them, through the preaching of the Gospel, they received and embraced him, and they loved Him because of His perfections, because of His person, and because He first loved them; they loved Him because of the fulness of grace that was in Him, because of what He had done for them, and because of the sufferings He endured for them, their love was spiritual; it was a fruit of the Spirit of God in their souls; was accompanied with faith in Christ, and proceeded from them receiving the Gospel in their hearts.

"and even though you do not see him now, you believe in him", believing not merely what He said, or did, or does, or will do; but looking on Him, and to Him, for life and salvation; embracing Him by faith, leaning upon Him as their Saviour and Redeemer; committing their all to Him, expecting all true goodness from Him, both grace and glory: and so *are filled with an inexpressible and glorious joy.*

This speaks of being filled with a joy in believing in Him, a joy that entirely passes our understanding, and it is a joy that is glorious and cannot be found in anything or anywhere or anybody else *for you are receiving the goal of your faith, the salvation of your souls*

They rejoiced in the salvation they received, but did not deserve.

What of us?

Can we say that though we have not seen Him, we love Him; and even though we do not see Him now, we believe in Him and are filled with an inexpressible and glorious joy, for we are receiving the goal of our faith, the salvation of our souls ?

Do we want historical proof about Jesus?

It is there not just in the Bible but in the writings of Jews and Romans who hated Him.

Do we need proof of our own sin and our need of salvation?

The proof is easily found in honest self-examination of our thoughts, our actions and our motivations.

The "goal of our faith" means, the object to which our faith is directed.

Faith has a content - Jesus our Saviour!

The salvation of our souls is accomplished for us by Jesus.

Matthew 20:28 *"The Son of Man did not come to be served, but to serve, and to give his life as a ransom for many."*

He is God in the flesh, who came alongside us, became one of us. He experienced our hurts, temptations, our human nature

He became weak, poured himself out, became vulnerable for us. He chose to live by faith as a human - God in human form, crucified as a common criminal, died, buried, raised, so that we may be forgiven, spiritually healed and restored! Restored to fellowship with our God!

Joy is not a fleeting emotion. It is a growing conviction of what God has done and will do for us, even though we deserve none of it. This is the realisation of God's grace. His favour towards undeserving sinners who repent of their sins and turn to Him to be forgiven and to be lifted!

So we come to the heart of real joy. We find joy in the Person of Jesus. We find joy in the Salvation of Jesus. We find joy in the Promises of Jesus. We find joy in the works of Jesus. We find joy in the accomplishments of Jesus. We find joy with Jesus in our hearts and lives.

What joy it is to know that my wife and my two sons love and know our Lord Jesus and live lives that serve Him in different ways.

We find joy in Almighty God. We find joy in the love of God. We find joy in the power of God. We find joy in our relationship with God. We find joy in God's Word. We find joy in prayer. We find joy with other believers. We find joy in praying with other believers.

Even when life is very tough, whether through illness or fear or disappointment or persecution or being let down by others, there can be joy in our Lord. That does not mean we will have earthly happiness all the time. That does not mean that we won't be anxious or annoyed at times. It does mean that we can fully rely on God and the salvation won for us in and by our Lord Jesus Christ.

It also means we can learn about joy in the Bible. Read the book of Philippians. Read about Ezra, in Nehemiah chapter 8, reading the law to the people for the first time in many, many years.

It means we can find joy in proper proclamation preaching of the full truth of God's Word. It means we can find joy in individual and collective prayer (I do not apologise for repeating this!). It means we can find joy in hymns and worship songs with deep, meaningful words. It means we can find joy in helping others. Real joy is not frivolous, it is deep. Real joy is not about nonsense, it is about truth and a relationship with the living God.

How sensible is it for us to believe in a God we cannot see with our eyes?

It is supremely sensible, because we can have a real, spiritual relationship with Him and that is essential to having balance and real joy in our lives!

CHAPTER 11
BALANCING ACT – CONTINUING TO REVIEW

Balance in the Christian life is not something we find and then it becomes fixed. We change. Our circumstances change. The world changes. Part of finding appropriate balance in the Christian life is to continually review and adapt to change. Indeed Christians who do not change will not merely stagnate but go backwards. We will not find balance as something comfortable and unchanging but as something that develops and grows and deepens. Balance is in finding how we can enjoy God's Creation, enjoy God's mercy, enjoy knowing God, enjoy learning from and about God, and enjoying serving God.

How do we serve God?

2 Peter 3:17-18 - *"Therefore, dear friends, since you have been forewarned, be on your guard so that you may not be carried away by the error of the lawless and fall from your secure position. But grow in the grace and knowledge of our Lord and Saviour Jesus Christ. To him be glory both now and forever! Amen."*

Part of working for appropriate balance in our Christian lives is to ask God to grow us in grace. This helps us to serve God better. What does this mean in practice?

Firstly, let us be clear that balance in the Christian life does not necessarily mean being down the middle in everything. This is especially so in terms of how seriously we take our faith in God and service to Him. It is not achieving balance in the Christian life if we are moderate, average, lukewarm, insipid and half-committed. The Church of Jesus Christ must not become a compromise or a crowd-pleasing enterprise. It offends God deeply if we dilute the truth of His Word or deny some parts of it. We must proclaim the whole truth knowing it will offend many because they refuse to face up to their own sins and the consequences of their own sins. Mealy-mouthed Christianity that 'does not rock the boat' is a supreme insult to our Saviour who gave His body and blood for us.

Jesus did not do a moderate job to solve our sin problem. He was not half-hearted. He died in our place, suffering physically, morally and spiritually for us. He balanced taking the punishment for our sin with giving believers the protective gift of His righteousness. This was whole-hearted balance. Remember this phrase - whole-hearted balance - and aim for it in our Christian lives. I repeat again, aim for whole-hearted balance!

Secondly, we need to continually reflect on and review our relationship with God. Are we faithful daily in Bible reading and prayer? Are we offering ourselves in service to God so that He can use our gifts to the furtherance of His kingdom? With the strength and guidance of the Holy Spirit, are we developing discernment in both the things of this world and the things of God, including realising how these two sets of things can be intermingled without compromising the truth of God's message?

Are our lives characterised by integrity and faithfulness? Do we say what we mean, mean what we say, and carry out all promises?

We are either Christians or we are not. Being a follower of Jesus is not a part-time occupation that we pick up when it suits us. 'Hold on Jesus, until I deal with this other priority in my life' is no way to repay Him for what He has done for us. This does not mean we have to be 'religious' all the time but it does mean that Jesus and His Word are top priority.

Are we concerned regularly with our spiritual development and that of others? The words of Paul are helpful here.

Ephesians 3:14-19 - *"I bow my knees before the Father, from whom every family in heaven and on earth is named, that according to the riches of his glory he may grant you to be strengthened with power through his Spirit in your inner being, so that Christ may dwell in your hearts through faith— that you, being rooted and grounded in love, may have strength to comprehend with all the saints what is the breadth and length and height and depth, and to know the love of Christ that surpasses knowledge, that you may be filled with all the fullness of God."*

Thirdly, assess how attached we are to the things of this world. It is not wrong to have pleasure in some of the things of this world if they do not harm us or others, but how do we know when they bring harm in more subtle or indirect ways?

Here is a key question for us to consider.

Do our worldly pleasures ever replace God in our heart? Added to this we can also ask ourselves if we flaunt worldly success or wealth or position instead of glorifying God and spreading His truth?

Truth means God's Truth, not a false version that fits in with the latest styles that are acceptable to other people.

We need to be in this world, part of it, experiencing it, but not ruled by it. How do we know if our "pleasures" are taking up too much of our lives? Examine our heart - is God first or are the "pleasures" first?

Is God our chief pleasure? Do we delight in His Word? Do we delight in speaking to others about Him? Are we seeking to know Him more? Is there evidence in our lives that God is developing our discernment so that we can judge what is right and do it even if it is not at all what our sinful nature wants to do?

2 Peter 3:18 *" But grow in the grace and knowledge of our Lord and Saviour Jesus Christ. To him be glory both now and forever! Amen."*

© **John Noble 2020**

THE AUTHOR

John Noble was brought up by Christian parents and he became a Christian at the age of 15. Born in Fraserburgh, he has also lived in Annan, Lockerbie, Aberdeen, Banchory and Peterhead. He graduated from Aberdeen University and developed a growing reputation and respect for his outstanding work in education, his work for God, his integrity and his strength of character.

He worked as a Teacher, an Assistant Principal Teacher, a Principal Teacher, an Assistant Head Teacher, an Education Officer, a Depute Head Teacher and a Head Teacher in secondary schools in the North-East of Scotland for nearly 35 years.

He has studied and taught theology and been a powerful Christian preacher for even longer, preaching in churches of various denominations to deliver a clear, exegetical and evangelical message of salvation through Jesus Christ.

As a Head Teacher he was renowned for his very firm but very fair discipline, his vision, his quick analytical thinking, his motivational speaking skills and his compassion.

John has also been a champion bowler, winning well over 200 trophies including many club and district championships and appearing in Scottish Finals.

He is very grateful for the Godly support of his loving wife Elizabeth, his sons John-William and Graeme and their wives Binglin and Avalin. These five people have been a joy in his life for many reasons but chiefly for the times they have together talking about their Saviour, God's Word and how to apply it to their lives through their Christian faith.

In terms of theological influences his late father-in-law Rev. William Brown would be at the top of the list that also includes his wife and sons plus books such as (some of) Louis Berkhof's Systematic Theology. However, he has never copied any influence but has assimilated, analysed and applied these influences with reference to how the Holy Spirit has led him to interpret God's Word. He continues to preach God's Word with knowledge, passion, enthusiasm and conviction, both in his own church Grace Baptist Church Aberdeen and elsewhere.

His first book, "How Do We Know Who We Really Are?" (2018) explored questions of human identity and how we can only truly find ourselves fully in a relationship with Jesus. This second book looks at how we can realistically put our relationship with God into practice in today's complex world, much of which seems to pull us away from God. John hopes that by reading this book we will reflect upon how we can live as part of this world without compromising our wonderful Saviour Jesus Christ.

Lightning Source UK Ltd.
Milton Keynes UK
UKHW012358130820
368212UK00001B/35